50 Ideas to Engage Student Writers

Cross-Curricular
Activities That Make Writing Fun

by Linda De Geronimo
and Anne Diehl

Grades 3-5

Carson-Dellosa Publishing Company, Inc.
Greensboro, North Carolina

Credits

Editor: Kelly Gunzenhauser

Layout Design: Jon Nawrocik

Cover Design: Matthew Van Zomeran

Cover Photographs: © 2001 Brand X Pictures

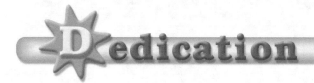

Dedication

For our children Bobby, Diana, Craig, David, Angie, and Lee, and our grandchildren Makenna and Eve.

Printed in the USA • All rights reserved.

ISBN 0-88724-276-6

Table of Contents

Introduction

More than ever, students need to learn to write well. They are being required to use the writing process at earlier ages and more frequently, and many school systems now incorporate some form of required writing test. In the face of standardized test preparation and larger classes, finding time to incorporate interesting and effective writing lessons into daily routines can be challenging.

With the fun activities in *50 Ideas to Engage Student Writers*, you can turn any subject into a writing opportunity. Many language arts activities are included, as well as lessons that focus on writing about math, science, social studies, and even art and music. Some activities have cross-curricular applications. You may choose to use the activities to teach writing for its own sake, but many can easily be incorporated into existing units. These adaptable activities are excellent for creating writing practice for students who are resistant to writing.

Additionally, most activities include extensions. Each extension may include a work display or sharing idea, a further application for the main activity, a presentation suggestion, or a way to make the activity more challenging. Some extensions can also be used as stand-alone activities.

Several activities can be combined to create units. For example, have students complete Two Bad What? (page 13), Fairy Tales Continued (page 14), and Add a Chapter (page 16) together to form a literature-based writing unit. Or, use Comics Convention (page 22), All I Got Was This T-shirt! (page 23), I Know A Secret! (page 24), Here's What's News (page 26), and In My Opinion (page 28) to form a unit about different types of newspaper writing. Also, consider using the four Mini-Units to focus and connect students' writing experiences. Finally, the In My Opinion Rubric (page 29), Writing Process Checklist (page 61), and Editing Checklist (page 62) can be used as a unit to teach students how to evaluate their own and others' writing. Young students may need help learning how to use these three lessons, but once they are familiar with them students should find the lessons very helpful.

Because of its flexibility, *50 Ideas to Engage Student Writers* includes many more than fifty creative ideas. Regardless of how you choose to use this book, there should be at least one writing activity that appeals to each student.

Color Me a Writer

Purpose:

Students can work with words in different ways in order to prepare themselves for writing. Use this activity as a warm-up to get them thinking about descriptive language.

Color My Words

Give each student a selection of crayons in many different colors. Choose adjectives that students know but are not color-specific, such as *sticky, hot, gooey, lazy, frigid, isolated,* etc. Say each adjective one at a time, and have each student choose an appropriate color for each adjective and color a shape around the word. (Any shape is fine.) Say about 10 adjectives. On a separate sheet of paper, have each student write about why he chose a particular color and shape for each adjective, and what the adjective reminds him of. Let a few volunteers share their answers for each adjective.

Next, have each student choose three adjectives from the list and write them at the top of a piece of writing paper. Instruct him to think about something that the three words together could describe, then write a descriptive paragraph using all three words. Have each student draw and color a picture of his paragraph. Post the writing and illustrations on a bulletin board covered with colorful paper.

Color Code

Let each student think about her favorite color. Provide colorful pens and pencils and let her write—in that color—why it is her favorite. Have students consider questions such as, "What does this color remind you of?" and "What objects are this color?" Repeat the activity with students' least-favorite colors. Share your own responses, as well.

Write Like the Wind

Language Arts

Purpose:

Freewriting sometimes produces students' best writing because there is no wrong way to write. Encourage students to free write often so that they experience how fun and easy writing can be.

Feel Free to Write

To create a different atmosphere and change the routine, consider playing different types of music during freewriting time. Let students choose from the following prompts and allow sufficient time for them to free write. When a student writes about an event or a memory that he treasures, his writing may become more descriptive and interesting. If they are willing, have students share their writing with their classmates but don't offer this option every time since freewriting is not necessarily meant to be shared with an audience.

- The day I learned to swim
- My first sleepover
- My favorite holiday
- My chorus performance
- Our championship game
- My new pet
- My best birthday
- If I were the teacher
- If I were the president
- The best/worst day I ever had

- The day I learned to ride a two-wheeled bicycle
- My favorite relative
- The luckiest thing that ever happened to me
- My band performance
- My student council election speech
- My trip to the beach/mountains/country/city/amusement park
- If I were the principal
- If I were my parents

Perfect Prompts

Sometimes prompts do not spark students' imaginations. Tell students to write "Better Prompt Challenge" cards. Before freewriting time, have students write their ideas on index cards and present them to you for approval.

Describe It!

Language Arts

Purpose:

When explaining descriptive writing to students, teachers usually tell students that readers should be able to see, feel, taste, and smell in their minds what the writer is describing. This is a tough idea for students to grasp. Make it real by having them create (and eat!) their own sandwich writing projects.

Eat Your (Descriptive) Words

Any popular sandwich items will work for this activity, but fun and unusual ones will make the writing more descriptive. Some suggested sandwich items are a few types of bread, peanut butter, jelly, marshmallow fluff, sliced bananas and apples, raisins and other dried fruit, and honey. Be sure to get parents' permission and information about food allergies and religious or other food preferences before completing this activity.

Next, set up an assembly line and have students create their own sandwiches, then return to their desks. As they eat their sandwiches, have students jot down words that describe them. Then, have each student write a descriptive paragraph (not a list of ingredients) about her delicious sandwich. Tell students that you want their classmates to be able to imagine taking a bite of each sandwich.

What's in Your Sandwich?

When students are finished eating, have them sign their papers and exchange them with classmates. After each student reads a new paper, have him write a list of ingredients he thinks were in the sandwich. Have students return the papers and lists and see if their descriptions helped their classmates guess correctly.

Sad Sandwich

Have students describe their sandwiches as if they were the worst sandwiches they had ever eaten. (Maybe some of them were!) Discuss how the adjectives would change. Have each student compare both paragraphs and explain which was the most descriptive and why.

Stupendous Sentences

Purpose:

One valuable lesson students can learn about writing is how to change their simple sentences into more complex, interesting sentences. Provide practice while creating a story.

Add-a-Sentence Story

Students should have paper and pencils available before they begin. Explain that they will write a story together. Set the tone of the story by writing the first sentence and reading it aloud. For example, write, "It seemed impossible, yet it was so quiet in the forest; it was as though every insect, animal, and plant was sleeping." Ask for a volunteer to write the next sentence. Explain that the volunteer must put the number two next to it and save it for later. Have the next volunteer write sentence number three, and so on. Remind students that the story should have a beginning, middle, and end. Continue until the story is finished and the sentences are numbered in order.

Ask students to look at their completed sentences and add adjectives, adverbs, and prepositional phrases to make them more interesting without changing the content. Model this with a few sentences so that students understand exactly what you want them to do. For example, change, "Then, a boy heard a noise," to "Suddenly, the frightened little boy heard a rustling noise right next to him."

When students are finished, make sure their sentences make sense in the story. If not, work as a group to revise them. Finally, ask for a volunteer to type the story on a computer while other students create pictures for the story. Ask for a volunteer to read the finished story aloud as you show the pictures.

Story Banner

To share the story with the school, make a bulletin board book. Post pieces of chart paper on a wall in a hallway. Write the sentences at the bottoms of the papers, grouping sentences that can be illustrated together. Let students draw pictures on each "page" to go with the story and add page numbers.

Window Writing

Language Arts

Purpose:

A picture prompt helps students write more descriptively. For this activity, students will need windows to write stories.

 **ctivity**

Throw Writing Out the Window

Explain that you will direct students' attention to a specific place and that you will ask questions about that place. Then, have students look out of the nearest windows. If students must move to do this, try to allot just five students per window so that they are not too crowded. Ask the following questions, allowing time for students to write their answers before moving on to the next one.

- What do you see? Describe the setting. Be sure to include as many details as possible.
- Who or what is outside of the window? Describe the characters. Remember that there are animals, birds, and insects that may not be visible but are present.
- Are you a character in the story or just a narrator?

- What are the characters doing? If you can't see them, make it up.
- Do you see a problem? Can you imagine one? Write a problem that could happen outside of the window.
- What is the solution to the problem?
- How does this story end? Is it happy? Sad?

When students have looked out of the windows, give them ample time to develop their stories. Tell students that they can change their stories as they write them. Students should use the Writing Process Checklist (page 61) to complete this assignment. Encourage students to keep looking out of the windows and to draw pictures of their stories. Share finished stories with the class.

 **xtension**

Story Graph

Discuss how different each story is even though students used the same scene. Use a Venn diagram or a bar graph to examine what is similar in stories and what is different. Elements could be type of problem, number of characters, gender of characters, happy or sad ending, etc.

Poetry Writing

Language Arts

Purpose:

Students should be exposed to poetry because it helps develop language skills. It also encourages them to express their knowledge about different subjects in a unique way. Immerse students in activities that require them to listen to poems, then write and read their own.

Center Idea

Poets' Corner

Make poetry a reward for students. Separate the poetry area from the rest of the classroom by hanging a curtain or turning a desk around. Stock books such as *Where the Sidewalk Ends* by Shel Silverstein (HarperCollins, 1975), *Love That Dog* by Sharon Creech (HarperTrophy, 2003), *If You're Not Here, Please Raise Your Hand* by Kalli Dakos (Aladdin, 1995), *Joyful Noise: Poems for Two Voices* by Paul Fleischman (HarperTrophy, 1992), etc. Give each student a folder to decorate and label as her poetry storage folder. Keep folders in the center and send them home at the end of the school year.

Activities

Types of Poems

Spend a week or two at the beginning of the year introducing several types of poetry to students. Then, at the beginning of each month, reintroduce one form of poetry with examples and have students use this type for one assignment. (Allow students to choose different types of poems for other assignments.) By the end of the year, many types of poetry should have been used.

Know the Lingo

Have students keep vocabulary sheets in their folders to learn poetry terminology. Introduce students to terms such as *line*, *stanza*, *verse*, and *rhyming pattern*. Then, use the activity below and those on page 11 to direct students toward specific types of poetry.

Acrostic Action

This non-rhyming poem starts with a name or word written vertically. Each line begins with a letter in that name or word. The lines should relate in some way to the person or word. Students enjoy writing acrostics about themselves, but consider having them write acrostic poems about you! Collect their poems. In response, write an acrostic for each student and return the papers.

Ballad

This poem, written in four-line stanzas, tells a story. Most of the time, only the second and fourth lines rhyme. Read a few passages from a ballad to demonstrate. Suggest that ballads are traditionally sad. Then, have each student choose a story she has written to retell in ballad format.

Cinquain

This type of poem is structured and does not rhyme. It has a specific number of syllables in each line as well as a specific idea in each line. Tell each student to choose a pet or animal and write a cinquain about it. Use the following poem to demonstrate or write one of your own.

Line	Syllables	Ideas	Example
1	2	noun	Beagle
2	4	adjectives	speckled, loyal
3	6	verbs with -ing	baying, running, leaning
4	8	phrase about the subject	He wants all of my attention.
5	2	synonym for line 1	Oscar

Haiku and Senryu

This type of poem has three non-rhyming lines and 17 syllables total: five in the first line, seven in the second, and five in the last. Haiku are usually about nature, while senryu can be about any subject. Inspire haiku by taking students outside on a beautiful day. Challenge each student to find one object and write three haiku about it without naming the object. Return to the classroom and let each student read his first poem while students try to guess the object. If no one guesses, let the student continue to read his poem until someone guesses the object or until the reader has to reveal it.

Limerick

In this five-line, funny poem, lines one, two, and five rhyme, and lines three and four rhyme. There is also a pattern of stressed syllables, or string beats. Have students write limericks about themselves that start with, "There once was a girl named (insert student's name here)" and tell silly stories about themselves. Make up your own example: "There once was a teacher named Miss White,/ Who wanted to turn out the light./ She flipped off the switch,/Made her bed in a ditch,/And she slept there the rest of the night."

Quatrain

This four-line stanza poem has three different rhyming patterns: either aabb, abab, or abba. Challenge each student to write a quatrain in one of the rhyme schemes. For example, an aabb poem might be: "I will plant a maple tree./It will grow tall as can be./When its growing is all done,/I'll make syrup for everyone!" Then, have her change it to a new rhyme scheme, altering the words if necessary: "I will plant a maple tree./I'll watch it grow so tall./Then, I'll have syrup in the spring,/And color in the fall."

Year-Round Poetry Project

At the beginning of the year, have students brainstorm a list of famous people or holidays. Have each student choose one holiday or person to research, then tell each student to write about his subject using several different poetry formats. He should also illustrate the poems and store the final copies in his own poetry folder. On the class calendar, write each student's name on the date of his holiday or special person's birthday. Throughout the year, let students read their poems aloud on the appropriate dates.

Poetry-Writing Mini-Unit

My Favorite Show

Language Arts

Purpose:

When students are passionate about subjects, their writing often shows marked improvement. Many students enjoy favorite television shows. "Channel" this enthusiasm into student writing by having students "plug" their favorite shows to classmates.

Must-See TV

Begin by discussing your favorite television shows. Give reasons for your choices. Ask students to list their own favorite shows and have them write their reasons next to each show. During this time, walk around the room to check shows listed by students for age-appropriate content. Tell students that shows not written for children will not be discussed in class. Next, have each student narrow his list to one favorite show. Challenge him to write an episode for that show. Tell him that the characters must remain the same; however, he may bring in guest stars for his episode. Remind students that most fictional shows have beginnings, middles that have some sort of problem or dilemma, and conclusions in which the problems or dilemmas are usually solved. Explain that they do not have to write dialogue, only the events that will happen in their episodes. If you allow students to choose nonfiction shows, such as animal programs, game shows, or sporting events, have them describe what will happen during the course of the shows. Have students use the Writing Process Checklist (page 61) to complete this activity. Share episodes with the class.

What's My Line?

For more advanced students, use this opportunity to teach dialogue writing. Have students work in groups to complete this activity. After writing their stories, students should assign parts and write lines for each character. You may have to cut the running time of the episodes down from 30 minutes to 15. Monitor groups for appropriate content and dialogue. Finally, challenge students to memorize their lines, bring in props, and perform their shows for the class.

Two Bad What?

Language Arts

Purpose:

Changing a story to make it something completely new is called *innovation*. Students learn from it because they can concentrate on one element, and also because they have the benefit of the author's original to guide them in using good form and language. Using a picture book ensures that the lesson does not take too long and simplifies issues for students.

Feature New Creatures

Begin by reading *Two Bad Ants* by Chris Van Allsburg (Houghton Mifflin Co., 1988). Discuss the ants' behavior, where they traveled, and their perception of each place. Ask how the story would change if the places were different or if the animals were bees, dogs, beavers, etc. Then, tell students they will rewrite the story using the same style of language, but they should use different animals as the main characters. Remind them to think about how the new insects' or animals' perceptions would be different. Let students do minor research about animal behavior if necessary. For example, bees live in hives and are small, so their reactions might be similar to those of the ants. A solitary animal, such as a tiger, might have a negative reaction to being around another tiger.

When students have completed the activity, allow them to create picture books with the same size and number of pages as your copy of *Two Bad Ants*. Have them copy their stories and illustrate them, then share them with the class. Discuss how each pair of animals reacted differently and why.

A Different Destination

Instead of the above activity, or in addition to it, leave the ants the same but change their destinations. For example, ask, "Would ants react differently to a candy factory or a maple tree farm?"

Other Innovative Innovations

Use other children's books by Van Allsburg for this activity. Let students change the animals in *Jumanji* (Houghton Mifflin Co., 1981), or have students change the train to a plane, the bell to another object, the boy to his parents, or Christmas to another holiday in *The Polar Express* (Houghton Mifflin Co., 1985).

Fairy Tales Continued

Language Arts

Purpose:

Even older students will enjoy this writing assignment because of their familiarity with the topic and a chance to write something funny. This activity will encourage students to write new stories about what happens the next day, after the "happily ever after."

After Happily Ever After

Gather several fairy tale picture books for this lesson. As a class, brainstorm a list of fairy tales and write them on a piece of chart paper. Explain to students that they will choose a fairy tale to continue. To model this lesson, gather students into a circle like they did in the lower grades and read a version of *Goldilocks and the Three Bears* aloud. Follow by reading *Goldilocks Continued* (page 15). Then, discuss how it feels to have a fairy tale continued. Ask students if they enjoyed the continuation. How would they have made it different? Ask if they have ever wanted a story to continue instead of ending.

Next, have students choose fairy tales and read the picture books before prewriting. Students should follow the Writing Process Checklist (page 61) to complete this story. Have students who finish early draw pictures to accompany their stories. Then, group students by fairy tale to read the original aloud, then read their continuations.

Act It Out

Let students return to their groups and read each other's endings, then select one to act out. Students can read their parts but should still use motion for emphasis. Invite a younger class to watch the shows.

New Nursery Rhymes

If the schedule does not permit the fairy tale activity, have students choose different nursery rhymes, such as "Mary Had a Little Lamb," "Old King Cole," "Hickory Dickory Dock," "Little Jack Horner," "Jack and Jill," etc., and write additional verses.

Goldilocks Continued

Goldilocks ran to her room when she got home. She plopped down on her bed, which was just right, and fell asleep only to have a bad dream. In her dream, Goldilocks and her parents were sitting down to enjoy their dinner when the doorbell rang. Goldilocks was surprised to see two police officers standing there.

"Are you Goldilocks?" one of the officers inquired.

"Why yes," she replied.

"You are under arrest for trespassing, stealing, and damage to property!" the second officer announced.

"Nooooo!" screamed Goldilocks.

"Wake up, dear, you're having a bad dream. It's dinnertime." said Goldilocks' mother as she gently shook her daughter.

Throughout dinner Goldilocks thought about her dream. She began to feel very guilty for what she had done. For the rest of the evening, Goldilocks planned how she would apologize to the three bears the following day.

Early the next morning, Goldilocks dressed and emptied her piggy bank. She went into town and bought steaming hot porridge, a tiny rocking chair, and a jar of honey. She carried her purchases through the woods to the house of the three bears.

Goldilocks put her packages down and rang the doorbell. Papa Bear answered the door and frowned as soon as he saw Goldilocks.

"Please, sir, I would like to apologize for my behavior yesterday. I have brought presents to replace the things I broke," stammered Goldilocks.

" Oh, well then, please come in," said Papa Bear. Goldilocks entered the house and placed her packages on the living room floor.

Goldilocks apologized to Papa Bear first, then Mama Bear, and lastly to Baby Bear. Goldilocks handed the hot porridge to Mama Bear, the new chair to Baby Bear, and the jar of honey to Papa Bear. The three bears thought that Goldilocks was so brave to return to their house that they invited her to stay and eat porridge with them.

Goldilocks and the three bears became good friends and saw each other often after that. They really did live happily ever after.

Add a Chapter

Purpose:

Creative writing is challenging to teach because some students have difficulty trying to think of something to write. In this activity, students' enthusiasm for the subject will solve this problem.

Chapter Challenge

Use students' enthusiasm for popular children's literature to teach creative writing. Poll your class to brainstorm a list of students' favorite chapter books. Lead a discussion about the most popular books. Assign students to groups according to books they have read, and have them brainstorm and list their favorite and least favorite parts.

Next, explain that each student will have an opportunity to add a chapter to a favorite book. The characters will remain the same, but students may add new ones for their chapters. Their chapters may come at the beginnings, middles, or ends of the stories. Explain that this is a chance for them to change things that happened in the books that they did not like, to enhance things that they did like, or perhaps to create something totally new. If possible, have students complete the group brainstorming assignment on one class day, then let students bring copies of their books to class to complete the writing assignment on the next day. Finally, let students rejoin their groups and read their added chapters to each other.

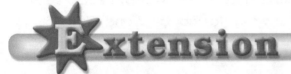

Whole New Book

Students may also enjoy adding new books to an existing series. Let each student choose a series and create a plot outline for the next book in the series. Explain that students may use the existing characters and also may add new ones. Note that some books in children's series are self-contained, such as those in the *Magic Tree House* series by Mary Pope Osborne (Random House Books for Young Readers, Random House Children's Books), meaning that there is a new story in each book, while other series have books that continue one story line through all of the books, as in the *Harry Potter* series by J. K. Rowling (Scholastic, Inc.).

Writing Object

Purpose:

Students often run out of ideas for writing good stories. Challenge them to create stories from pictures but with unusual guidelines. The pictures should stir their imaginations and help them to produce creative and original stories.

Activity

Picture Prose

Prior to this activity, cut out interesting pictures of objects, such as a spoon, lollipop, tree, bicycle, mountain, etc., from various magazines. Try to limit the number of objects in each picture. Give each student a picture and explain that his job is to write a story about a land where no one has ever been before, that uses something from that picture. Perhaps a story could be about a land where spoons live or the adventures of a lollipop. Remind students to use descriptive words when describing their characters and settings. Also, remind them that a story must have a beginning, middle, and end. Let students use the Writing Process Checklist (page 61) to help them write their stories.

After students have written their stories, have them convert the stories to picture books for younger children. They should decide how to break up their writing into pages and consider what type of picture would go with each group of sentences or paragraph. This is an excellent time to tell students to evaluate whether their stories are descriptive enough. Do they need to add words or sentences to match the pictures they have drawn? Or, do they need to add more details to the pictures?

Extension

Print Shop

Have students use computers to print their stories for their picture books. This will give them practice with word-processing skills as well as help with spacing for the different pages of their books. Allow them to glue their pictures to the tops of pieces of construction paper and glue the printed words at the bottoms. Encourage them to experiment with different fonts and sizes to create fun pages and covers.

I Will Survive!

Language Arts

Purpose:

Creating a scenario and mood for students can inspire their creativity. Have students use prior knowledge and life experience to create survival plans, first on rafts and then on deserted islands. They will assess the situations, determine immediate and long-term needs, and set goals.

Activity

Sole Survivor

Brainstorm a list of survival needs (food and water, shelter, clothing, safe environment, etc.). Turn down the lights and perhaps play a recording of ocean sounds. Have each student imagine she is on a family vacation in Hawaii. Discuss how the islands were formed and list their vegetation, climate, geography, animals, and insects. State that each student is floating on a raft in the Pacific Ocean, and it is so relaxing that she falls asleep. Have students listen to you read Part One and write about how they would survive for at least five days on rafts. After students have completed Part One, assign Part Two.

Part One: This Must Be a Nightmare! You wake up and realize that you are lost at sea! You do not know how long you have been sleeping or where you are. You have on a swimsuit (and shorts, if you are a girl), sneakers, and a pair of wire-framed sunglasses. In the raft, you have a can of soda, a peanut butter and jelly sandwich wrapped in foil, a bag of potato chips, and a towel. How will you survive? Write an essay describing the steps you would take to survive on this raft for at least five days. Remember that you will get very hungry, dehydrated, and sunburned. Decide how to use your supplies to save yourself.

Part Two: Land Ho! After five days on your raft, you spot land. You paddle your way to the island. It is deserted. You pull your raft onto the beach and begin to explore. You find bananas, coconuts, pineapples, and many different animals (lizards, fish, bats, birds, etc.). Write about how you will survive on this island. Describe your surroundings and how you will try to be rescued, set short and long-term goals for survival, and describe your results after a week, a month, and a year.

Extension

Rescued at Last

Have each student write a third story about how he was rescued and what he did when he got home.

Let's Play!

Language Arts

Purpose:

Giving directions or writing rules for something can be challenging for students because they must be clear, organized, and precise. Students who do not use prewriting usually have a difficult time achieving these goals. Direct students to complete a specific prewriting activity to ensure greater success.

Playing Games

Begin by having students list their favorite sports or games to watch on television or to play. Then, tell students that a new (pretend) student from another country is entering the class and wants to learn how to play the games and sports. The assignment is to explain how to play each game. Before students get started with the explanations, have them write the following headings on sheets of paper. Read the accompanying explanations of each heading and answer any questions students may have.

Introduction: Write a brief explanation of the sport/game.
Objective: What do you have to do to play the sport/game well? Throw a ball in a basket? Throw the ball to a hitter? Answer questions correctly?
Players: How many players are on each team? What is the name and duty of each position?
Equipment: What equipment is needed to play?
Time: How long does this sport/game last? Are there quarters? Halves? Innings? Matches? No limit?
Playing Field: Where is this sport/game played? How large is the area?
Rules: What rules apply to this sport/game?
Penalties: Are there penalties in this sport/game? If so, what are they and how can they affect the outcome?

Game Time

Make this activity cooperative by grouping students according to the games or sports they choose. (Consider providing limited options so that every student will have a group.) Have students in each group write their directions together. Then, allow students to play some of the games.

Timed Writing

Language Arts

Purpose:

These activities will help students become more aware of allocated time, remaining time, and the amount of work they will be able to accomplish, especially when using the writing process during tests.

Prewriting Idea

Get Ready to Write

Students are often caught off guard when given a specific amount of time to complete a project. They become so involved in the project that they forget to check the clock. Practice giving students specific times to complete ordinary tasks. Some suggestions for these activities are cleaning out a desk or taking a bathroom break (five minutes), having a snack (10 minutes), researching on the Internet or completing a math word problem (15 minutes). Repeat activities often, increasing and decreasing times until students truly understand just how long increments of 5, 10, 30, or 45 minutes really are.

Activities

Counting the Minutes

Complete this activity in any subject area when students have a lesson that requires them to work in pairs. Select one student to be the timekeeper. Throughout the lesson, have the timekeeper give updates about how much time has elapsed. Switch timekeepers for a lesson on another day.

Count on Me

Have each student compile a list of things that he does at home and estimate how long it takes to complete each task. Some examples are getting ready for bed, eating breakfast, emptying the dishwasher, feeding a pet, playing a video game, etc. Direct students to time each listed activity they complete. Discuss the results. Did their estimated times match the actual times? How far off were their estimates? Did they do things faster knowing they were timing themselves? Did they realize that they complain about chores that don't take very long to complete? Try this activity again with a new list to see if their estimates are now more accurate.

No Time to Waste

Discuss with students how short commercials are. If possible, watch a few in class and time them. Ask each student to write a 30-second commercial for a favorite toy, candy, etc. Time students with a stopwatch as they perform their commercials. Students must stop immediately when time is up. Challenge them to persuade the audience to buy their products in the time given. Repeat this activity with one-minute commercials.

Concealed Clock

Wear a watch to class and cover the clock in your classroom for one day. Throughout the day, ask students to write down what time they think it is and to number their guesses. Make a list of your own with the correct times. At the end of the day, reveal the real times. Have students write math problems to show how close their guesses were.

Paragraph Punctuality

Give students a paragraph topic they can easily write about, such as what they are doing over the weekend or what they think they might have for lunch. Let them write for as long as they want, then write down the times when they finish. (Assign another task to complete after this activity so that students who finish quickly are not waiting and slow finishers do not feel rushed.) Collect the papers and evaluate how thorough and complete the writing is in relation to the amount of time each student spent writing. Use this as an assessment to help students organize their thoughts more quickly and write more thoroughly on a timed writing test. Repeat the activity several times to assess whether students improve.

Fast Write

Choose a curriculum-related topic that lends itself to quick writing, such as listing favorite foods, writing as many words as possible that begin with a certain letter, listing as many verbs as possible, etc. Tell students that they have five minutes to complete the assignment. Reward the student with the most correct items listed. Periodically assign this exercise, but increase the time and make the assignment more complex each time until students write for 45 minutes.

Timed Writing Process

Some timed writing tests allot a portion of the time for process writing. Help students practice condensing this process. Review the Writing Process Checklist (page 61). Break down how much time students should use for each step. For example, in a one-hour test, suggest that students use five minutes for brainstorming and other prewriting, 15-20 minutes for drafting, 15-20 minutes for revising, and the rest of the time for editing and publishing. Explain that if students mark their editing mistakes and then address them as they rewrite, they can combine the editing and publishing steps. Next, give a timed writing assignment. Inform students when they should move to the next step in the process. Discuss how they feel they did when the assignment is over and evaluate their papers. Repeat this activity several times until students are familiar with the format.

Timed Writing Mini-Unit

Comics Convention

Language Arts

Purpose:

Students usually love to read comics, so provide the opportunity for them to write and illustrate their own with a focus on dialogue. This activity also helps students learn to visualize as they read and write.

Writing the Funnies

Introduce dialogue writing by showing students samples of comic strips. Discuss the speech balloons and explain that they contain the words being spoken by different characters in the comic. Highlight the difference between words that are spoken and words that are thought (in "thought balloons"). Discuss the conversation. Was it funny? Sad? And, how did the pictures contribute to the story? Then, use correction fluid to cover the dialogue in a familiar comic strip. Copy the strip without dialogue for students. Have students write what they think the characters are saying and share responses.

Finally, direct students to write their own comic strips. They can create characters of their own or use familiar characters. First, have each student write a story that she wants to tell. Then, have her take notes about what the drawings should look like and how she can use them to embellish the humor in the strip or to take the place of some of the dialogue. (Provide examples of comics where the illustrations are more important than the dialogue.) Next, instruct students to write rough drafts of their comics with simple sketches of characters. Review the comics and give feedback. Then, provide students with white construction paper for their final drafts. Instruct them to use rulers to create as many boxes and scenes as necessary and color the final strips to look like the comic strips in Sunday newspapers. Display the comics on a bulletin board using black and white newsprint as the background.

Curriculum Comics

Connect dialogue writing to other curriculum areas. Have students review major events or concepts by writing character dialogue about what happened. For example, a student could draw a strip about a firefighter explaining to a child what to do in case of a house fire or about Davy Crockett explaining the dangers of the wilderness to pioneers.

All I Got Was This T-shirt!

Purpose:

Make writing about summer vacation fun and different! Do this activity as a start-of-year icebreaker for students since it is often easier to answer questions in front of the class instead of reading a story or report.

The Shirt Says It All

Gather permanent markers, fabric paint, and samples of ads featuring vacation places. (A travel agency is a good source.) Also, ask each student to provide a plain, white T-shirt. (It is more fun for students if the shirts are real; however, students can cut T-shirt shapes from white bulletin board paper if necessary.)

Have students work in groups. Distribute a few advertising brochures to each group and have them discuss what makes a good advertisement. Direct students to notice the pictures, the sizes and number of words, and the colors and layout of each ad. Have one member of each group jot down ideas. Discuss students' findings as a whole class. On a piece of chart paper, list what students find are the important elements of a travel ad. For example, students may list things like easy-to-read print, colorful photographs of animals or people having a good time, clean layout, and special bonuses and rewards, such as children stay free, buy one night and get one free, admit two for the price of one, etc.

Next, let students create ads for their summer vacation spots or any places they have traveled. Let each student write and draw a rough draft on a sheet of paper, then recopy the final draft of the ad onto the T-shirt. (Students may use the fronts and backs depending on their designs.) Make sure each student knows to focus on one attraction or aspect of the vacation. When the shirts are dry, let each student wear his shirt and stand in front of the class to answer questions (rather than just report) about his vacation spot.

Open House Party

Create a bulletin board with the T-shirts to show parents on an open house or parents' night. If the shirts are large enough, let each parent leave the open house wearing her child's shirt.

I Know a Secret!

Language Arts

Purpose:

Students who seldom talk about themselves may be more comfortable sharing information in writing assignments. In this activity, students will use interviewing techniques to find out about each other. Perhaps students who seldom talked with each other will find they have something in common.

Activity

I Didn't Know That

Assign partners who do not know each other well. Explain that each student should interview his partner and find out something about her that other classmates do not know. Have a student use the I Know a Secret! reproducible (page 25) to conduct a model interview with you. Or, interview someone else in the school, such as the principal, and share the resulting written biography. After they have completed their interviews, direct students to write biographies about their partners, as well.

Extensions

Guess Who?

Have each student fill out the interview sheet privately. Randomly distribute the completed sheets, making sure no one gets her own sheet. Have each student write or speak about her person and have classmates try to guess who it is.

More Interview Prospects

Let students use their interview skills on others. Students can interview family members, friends outside of class, other teachers, or students in a younger classroom. Let students write reports about these interviews and share them with the class. Make sure that one student gets the opportunity to interview you since students are often curious about their teachers.

I Know a Secret!

Use these questions to help you do your interview.
Write the responses in the blanks provided.

Interview Reproducible

1. Name:_____

2. Age:_____ 3. I have ___ brothers and ___ sisters.

4. I live with my _____.

5. When I am not in school, I _____

   _____.

6. My favorite thing to do is _____.

7. My favorite place to be is _____.

8. My least favorite thing to do is _____.

9. My least favorite place to be is _____.

10. I am very good at _____.

11. I love to _____.

12. I wish I could _____.

13. I never want to _____.

14. When I grow up, I want to _____.

15. Few people know this about me, but _____

    _____.

Here's What's News

Language Arts

Purpose:

Students should be encouraged to read the newspaper to keep up with current events. Poll your class to find out how many students read the newspaper—you might be pleasantly surprised! If students become familiar with each part of the paper, they may be motivated to read more than just the comics.

Field-Day Fun

Supply newspapers for students. Consider contacting your local newspaper and asking them to donate copies. As a class, look at the different sections of the paper. Create a chart of sections, such as national news, state news, local news, arts and leisure, classified ads, and sports. Discuss what would be included in each section. Then, assign students to groups according to which section interests them most and ask each group to bring in articles from their section of the newspaper to report on in class. Continue this activity for a week. Switch sections and repeat until all groups are familiar with each newspaper section.

Culminate the activity by creating your own class newspaper organized around a school event, such as a field day, open house, multicultural night, etc. Assign an editor and an assistant editor, reporters, illustrators, layout artists, an advertising manager, couriers, and any other workers needed to successfully create, produce, and distribute your newspaper. Suggest topics for each section. For example, if students are reporting on a field day, the local news group could write about the events and about other school field days, the sports group could describe events and list scores, the arts group could report on posters used to advertise the field day, etc. Whether this project is a one-time event or continues on a monthly basis, students will be proud to deliver their newspapers to the rest of the school.

News at Six

If time is limited and creating an entire newspaper is too large a project for your class, assign different articles to groups of students. Have them work as a group to write copy so that one student in the group can give an oral report, then let them role-play reporting the story for a major news network.

What Would You Change?

Purpose:

With this activity, students will evaluate their school day and attempt to provide schedules they feel are more conducive to learning. They will have the opportunity to give feedback about their likes and dislikes, and also to practice persuasive writing.

Activity

If I Were the Teacher

Ask each student to evaluate her school day. If she were the teacher, would she continue the schedule in the same way? What would she change and why? What activities would she delete from the schedule, and what activities would she add to the schedule? Remind students that all subjects must still be taught (even the ones that aren't their favorites!).

Distribute blank daily schedules. Have each student jot down a few notes on scrap paper and then fill in the school day schedule as she would like it to happen. On the back of the paper, have her write reasons for each change in the schedule.

Share schedules with the class. Have the class vote on the best schedule and write their reasons for their choice. Implement some of their suggestions to show that you value their opinions.

Extension

If I Were the Principal

Have students write about changes to the school day that only the principal could change, such as lunch or recess times, dress code, etc. Combine ideas that everyone agrees with to create a master list of changes students would like to see in their school. Vote on one student to write a letter to the principal asking her to consider the changes for the following year. Ask for a response to the letter (at her convenience).

In My Opinion

Language Arts

Purpose:

Help each student learn to identify the components of an editorial, as well as write one of his own and assess someone else's. This activity gives students reasons to practice persuasive writing.

Editorializing

Discuss editorials and letters to the editor. Provide samples from a newspaper and ask students to do the same. Choose the topics carefully. Have students form groups and brainstorm the important elements that comprise an editorial, such as an attention-getting opening (maybe a personal experience), a specific opinion about an issue that affects many people, sentences to support that opinion, and a conclusion that sums up the important ideas in the editorial.

Next, bring the class together and use students' ideas to create a rubric for a good editorial. Students understand and take ownership of a rubric if they create it themselves. Use the sample rubric on the In My Opinion reproducible (page 29) to demonstrate or for students to add to. Have students brainstorm to find topics that interest them. List them on the board, then choose one issue and have the class write an editorial together. Use the rubric you have created to score your editorial.

Tell students that they will write editorials themselves. They should use the Writing Process Checklist (page 61) to complete this activity. Let students use the rubric to evaluate each other's papers. Finally, have students "publish" their editorials in a school newspaper or newsletter, or on a bulletin board.

Extra! Extra!

If your school does not publish a paper, create a classroom newspaper and publish the editorials there. For more information on creating a classroom newspaper, see page 26.

In My Opinion

Add to this rubric by scoring your paper, letting a friend score it, and then recording the score from your teacher. The points shown are the best possible score for each category, but you can award fewer points if necessary. Or, create your own rubric using this page as a model. Then, use it to score an editorial.

Editorial Rubric

Rubric Criteria		My Score	My Friend's Score	My Teacher's Score
The beginning is interesting and makes the reader want to read more.	5 points			
The topic is clear and of interest to many people, not just the writer.	5 points			
The sentences support the opinion on this issue.	5 points			
The conclusion sums up all of the important ideas.	3 points			
There are few, if any, spelling and grammatical errors.	2 points			

I Don't Want to Go to Bed!

Language Arts

Purpose:

Persuasive paragraph writing is often seen as a standardized test prompt. Each student is expected to clearly state his point of view, offer meaningful examples, and add a conclusion that sums up the key points of his argument. Turn practice for this type of essay into a personal assignment that has meaning for students.

Wish List Writing

Have students list things they might have wanted or wanted to do but were told no by their families. Have them include the reasons they were given for the answers. Make a wish list of students' requests on the board. Next to each request, list the possible objections. Discuss with students that in order to change their families' minds about something, they must think of answers to the objections. Read the following sample scenario:

- Juanita wants her bedtime changed from 8:30 PM to 9:00 PM.
- Juanita's parents say that she needs her rest in order to be a good student and so she won't be grouchy.
- Juanita says that she would like a trial period to prove that she is old enough to recognize when she is tired and mature enough to go to bed earlier if she thinks it is necessary. Juanita requests a month to prove to her parents that the extra half hour at night will not affect her schoolwork or her personality.
- Juanita reminds her parents that she stays up later in the summer when her schedule is much more strenuous with extra soccer practices, and she still gets her chores done and completes her summer reading with a great big smile on her face.

Then, have students brainstorm answers to some of their parents' objections. When they seem to understand the process, ask each student to write a letter to his family asking for something on his wish list. In the body of the letter, ask him to address his family's objections and give a reason or reasons why this request is a good idea. Review proper letter-writing format if necessary.

Extension

Here's How It Turned Out

If students' requests are reasonable and families are receptive, have students give letters to their families and ask for written responses. Let students share them with the class.

Math Riddles

Purpose:

Students like to write riddles and guess the answers to them, and riddles help students develop analytical skills. Introduce a math and writing lesson about riddles. Make up simple riddles like the examples below.

Riddle Dee Dee

Give a few oral and written examples of simple math riddles like the ones below. Stress that the "What am I?" question should be answered using the clues given in the five or six statements. Give students the following examples to solve.

I am larger than 10.
I am not divisible by 2.
I am less than half of 36.
I am prime.
The sum of my digits is 8.
What am I? (The number 17)

I am a two-digit number.
I am bigger than 25.
I am smaller than 40.
My ones digit is odd.
My tens digit is six less than
 my ones digit.
The sum of my digits is 12.
What am I? (The number 39)

After presenting a few number riddles, give students time to write number riddles of their own. Let each student share her best riddle with the class. Call on volunteers to solve the riddles.

Riddle Me This!

Riddle writing can be adapted to any curriculum area. Have students write riddles about what they are studying (plants, animals, etc.). For social studies, have students write riddles about historical figures. Or, let students choose curriculum areas. Use the riddles for test review.

What's the Answer?

Purpose:

This activity combines creative writing with math. If students complete a similar activity on a monthly basis, they may begin to look at word problems differently, perhaps like fun stories to solve.

Math Minder

Distribute copies of the story below. Instruct students to solve the math minders (word problems) at the end of the story and show the steps they use. Depending on students' levels, modify the story to include addition, subtraction, multiplication, division, fractions, percents, etc.

Jack's Shopping Day

Jack woke up early on Saturday. He knew he would be busy. After breakfast, he emptied his piggy bank and counted his money. He had saved $100.00. Jack asked his dad to drive him to the mall to do some holiday shopping. Jack was excited about presents he planned to buy for his family. The only one he couldn't buy that day was for his dad because his dad was with him. He would buy his dad a present when he went shopping with his mom. He knew that his dad's present would cost $29.00, so he had to remember to save that much money.

First, they went to the toy store. Jack bought a doll for his little sister. It was $10.00, but he had a coupon for $2.00 off. Next, he bought his older brother a video game that cost $25.00. He didn't have a coupon for it, but when he went to the register, he found out that the video game was on sale for $22.00. Jack was excited. Next, Jack went to a department store and went right up to the cosmetic counter. He knew his mom's favorite lotion, and he couldn't wait to buy it for her. There were two sizes of bottles and Jack stood there for a long time trying to decide which one he should buy. The four-ounce bottle was $35.00, but the eight-ounce bottle was $60.00. The eight-ounce bottle was a better deal and Jack really wanted it, but he didn't know if he had enough money.
Question: Does Jack have enough money to buy the eight-ounce bottle? The four-ounce bottle? Find out how much money Jack has left after his purchases and decide which bottle of lotion Jack can buy. After Jack's day of shopping, how much money will he have left? Don't forget that Jack has to save money for his dad's present. If there was a 5% sales tax on everything Jack bought, would he have enough money for his purchases?

After you discuss that Jack cannot buy the eight-ounce bottle, have students write more shopping problems for Jack. Does he decide to return a gift? What does he buy instead? Does he change his mom's or dad's present? Collect the new math minders and redistribute them for students to solve. Rather than check the new math minders for solvability, let students decide whether the problems will work, then share them with the class.

Let's Go Shopping

Purpose:

Estimation is an essential skill that requires practice. In this activity, students will use critical thinking skills to create lists of basic supplies and estimate their prices.

My Shopping List

Prior to this activity, ask students and staff to collect advertisements and receipts from grocery stores. Mark out any credit card numbers. Explain that each student should create a food-shopping list for a new home. Have students brainstorm items necessary to stock a new kitchen. Tell them to think about the items they and their families use on a daily basis. Remind students that some foods, like sweets or frozen pizza, are not basic necessities for a kitchen. Also, remind them that some food is perishable, so they should buy only what they can use in a short amount of time. After students have completed their lists, have them estimate the price of each item and use calculators to total their shopping lists.

Next, assign students to small groups. Give each group a stack of advertisements and receipts. Have them check their estimations and write the correct amount next to each item. Again, have students use calculators to total their lists. Compare their estimations to the actual amounts. Discuss the differences.

It's My Party

Have students use the same process to create new shopping lists for a holiday party. Compare and contrast students' estimates and actual amounts again. Were their estimates more accurate?

Field Trip

Have each student accompany a family member to a grocery store. Before the trip, ask family members to let the student estimate prices for shopping-list items, then allow him to check off each item as it is placed into the shopping cart and write down how much each item costs. Again, let students use calculators to compare their estimations and the actual prices. This time, let each student write about which items he estimated incorrectly. Is there a connection between the types of items and whether he over- or underestimates the prices?

Math Journals

Purpose:

The most difficult time students have when working in math classes usually involves solving math word problems and explaining how they solved them, especially when there are multistep solutions. Students may also have trouble explaining how they solved math problems that use only numerals. Give students the opportunity to write about math on a daily basis. Have students create journals just for math. When students regularly explain how to solve math problems in writing, they will better understand word problems and their apprehension about math and writing will decrease.

Center Idea

Math Magic

Take the intimidation factor out of math with a fun math center. Provide calculators, age-appropriate manipulatives, graph paper, colorful pencils, an abacus, protractors, tangrams, and fun math problems. Change items in the center according to what students are learning and make visits to the math center rewarding. Let students use the items in the center when they have in-class journal assignments or allow them to visit the center as a different place to write about math.

Activities

Math Is Useful

To help students understand that they need to be proficient in math like they are in reading, assign a family-child journal activity. Instruct each student to keep a record for 24 hours of when she uses any type of math, even counting. Most students will record looking at the clock, counting minutes until class is over, and using math in school. Send home a note requesting that a family member complete the same assignment. Remind families that knowing how much gas to pump, watching the speed limit, paying for items, counting subway stops, using an oven or microwave, and other everyday activities all involve math. Let students share both journals in class, then discuss other ways they will need to use math outside of school.

Math at Home

Each night, assign a word problem that is slightly more difficult and requires creative thinking. Encourage students to involve their parents when they don't understand how to solve it. (When such problems are assigned during class time, often only the brighter students will attempt to solve the problem while others give up.) After they have solved the problem, have students write the steps they used. For example, a simple math problem about how to fit 21 flowers in three rows could have an explanation like, "I had 21 flowers to plant, and I knew that I had room for only three rows. I drew a garden with three rows. I kept adding a flower to each row until I used all 21. I ended up with seven flowers in each row."

Math Journals Mini-Unit

Warm-Up Math

Use journals for a daily math warm-up. Have students practice counting things like the days of the month, then use ordinal numbers to write, "Today is the twenty-seventh day of January."

Wrap-Up Math

End each math lesson with a written review. Model written reviews for students until they are familiar with this procedure. "To find the mean of numbers you must first add the numbers. Next, count how many numbers you added and divide that number into your sum. Your answer will be the mean, or average of the numbers." You may want to have students use a separate section of their journals for this. If so, have students date their entries so that they will have a quick reference to refresh their memories.

Word Problem Starters

Give students a math problem and have them write word problems to match it. For example if you give the problem $200.00 – $15.00 = $185.00, a student may write, "Rashad went to buy a CD player. He had a coupon for $15.00 off the price of any CD player. The one he chose was $200.00. How much did Rashad pay for his CD player?"

Count Down to Fun

Have each student use her journal to count the days to her birthday or another special day. Make sure she writes the numbers with words in this way: My birthday is June fifth. There are one hundred fourteen days left until my birthday.

Math Memory

Have students use their journals to record reminders for themselves so that during homework time they can remember what was taught in class. For example, students learning about prime numbers may write, "Prime numbers are numbers that have only two factors, themselves and one. Two, five, seven, and eleven are prime. Remember: Nine's not prime! Nine's not prime!"

Measure Up

Measurement can be difficult for students. Write a list of objects on the board and ask students to write in their journals what units of measurement they could use to measure it. For example, for sugar, students could write cups, pounds, liters, ounces, teaspoons, etc. For a desk, students could write inches, feet, centimeters, pounds, etc. As students learn to choose units, add objects with more complicated options, such as an ice cube, the air in a balloon, etc.

Graph It!

Math

Purpose:

Students often enjoy graphing, and it makes math more tangible for visual learners. Use this activity after students have been introduced to line graphs, bar graphs, pictographs, and circle graphs, or modify it to suit students' skills.

Survey Says

Brainstorm ideas for a survey you would like to conduct with students, such as favorite ice cream, color of shoes worn that day, number of siblings, number of pets, types of sandwiches in their lunch boxes, etc. Write the question on the board and have students write the answers in their math journals. List responses on the board. Then, instruct each student to create a line graph, pictograph, bar graph, and circle (pie) graph with the results. (Adjust to accommodate graphs students know or use it as a teaching tool to introduce different types of graphs.) Have students write reports about the graphs, comparing them and answering these questions: "Which of your graphs do you like best? Why? Was this assignment easy? Why or why not? Which graph was the hardest to create? Why? Which graph was the easiest to create? Why? Which graph makes it easiest to read your results? Why? Did the number of people surveyed affect your graph in any way? If so, how would you change it next time? If you could change the way you created any of your graphs, what would you change? Would you like to try this again with another survey question? Why or why not?"

More Graph Fun

Make this graphing activity more word-oriented. Choose a seasonal or school-related word or phrase with at least eight letters, such as the name of your school. Tell students to make as many words as they can with the letters in that word. Stop them after five minutes so that the lists do not get too long. Next, list the words students made and tally the number of times each was used. Ask students to write about which type of graph would best represent the data and why. Then, collect the work and, as a class, create the type of graph most students want to use. (Depending on the number of words, either a circle or bar graph will probably work best.)

Wonderful Wives' Tales

Purpose:

Students need to practice critical thinking as much as they need to practice writing. In this activity, students will challenge themselves to discover the truth about wives' tales.

A Grain of Salt

Begin by discussing wives' tales with students and explain that these commonly held beliefs are sometimes based in truth. Have them brainstorm as many as they can, such as reading in dim light will ruin eyesight, if you go outside with wet hair you'll catch a cold, starve a fever and feed a cold, wait an hour after eating before swimming, carrots are good for your eyesight, chicken soup will make you well, etc. Write these on the board. Ask if students think they are true, and ask why or why not.

Next, have each student choose three wives' tales, write them down, and decide if there could be any truth to each. Have students write their responses next to the tales. Then, discuss the answers and point out if students have any reasons for validating the wives' tales that might be true. Finally, let each student research one of his tales, write whether it is true, and report back to the class.

Cliché Commentary

Clichés are similar to wives' tales in that they are often repeated as truth. Help students make a list of clichés, such as there is no use crying over spilled milk, a bird in the hand is worth two in the bush, a watched pot never boils, etc. Ask each student to choose one cliché, write about what it means, and give an example about how it applies to her life.

I'm Doing Well!

Purpose:

Self-reflection is a useful exercise, and writing about it is even better. Use this writing activity to focus on healthy habits.

Healthy Habits

Begin by explaining what you do to maintain your health. If you exercise or try to eat well, explain how. Tell students that being healthy is important and that many people take steps to ensure that they are in good shape. Have students think about things they might like to do to improve their health. Brainstorm a list of healthy activities, such as walk more each day, drink water instead of soda, eat more vegetables, brush teeth more often, etc. After you have brainstormed a list, help students choose activities to do for a week. You may have students do the activity together in class or individually at home. If all students do the activity together, choose something like exercise during recess or eat vegetables at snack time. If students choose different activities, make sure they are reasonable and easy for the student to follow. Have each student record when she does the activity, how well, and how it makes her feel. For example, if a student decides to eat a daily vegetable snack, she should write down the snack, how much she eats, at what time, and how she feels. She should also record if she eats a different snack instead.

At the end of one week, have each student write a reflection. Did she successfully complete the week's activity? Does she feel good or bad about it? What changes does she notice? Will she continue with the activity or do something different, or even add something else? Reward each student for her effort. If students are excited about reaching their goals, choose new goals and continue for a second week.

We Reached Our Goals!

If students continue to work on health and fitness goals, celebrate after several weeks. Bring in fruit and yogurt to make smoothies, and provide fun music to exercise to. Then, let students write about new goals they would like to set. Be sure to get parents' permission and information about food allergies and religious or other food preferences before completing this activity.

All About Organisms

Purpose:

Give students practice in recording data while maximizing the use of a science textbook. Each student will find an organism, observe it, draw it, record data, research it, and contribute to a class nature study guide.

Living Things

Have students research local animals and plants. Review the concepts of living and nonliving. Give students drawing paper, clipboards, and pencils, and take them outside to find living things to research, such as flowers, insects, trees, etc. Have each student quickly draw his organism and list observations about it. Remind each student to think about size, shape, color, etc. When students return to the classroom, let them first look up the organisms in their science books, then supplement their knowledge with other resources. (Use this opportunity to assess students' research abilities.) Using field notes and his research, have each student write a detailed, scientific description of his living thing in bullet format. For example, a student who has drawn a magnolia flower might make the following list:

- Large flowers (up to 12 inches across)
- Flowers often described as saucer-shaped
- Intense smell
- Flowers usually white
- Flowers grow on an evergreen tree.
- This tree grows best in the southern U.S.

Allow each student to draw a diagram of his organism and attach the written portion of the assignment to the illustration. Combine the descriptions and drawings on facing pages in a class nature book.

Show and Tell

Have each student show his page to a younger classroom and talk about her organism and where to find one on the school grounds.

Oh No! Aphids!

Formulate problems for students to solve. For example, ask questions like, "The flower is being attacked by aphids. What can a gardener do to save it?" Or, "A hive of bees is looking for a new home. How can they find one and what should they look for?" Have students write about the answers they find from the organisms' points of view.

I Can Help

Purpose:

Students should understand that every person makes a difference when deciding the future of our planet. Help students become aware of their ability to help the environment.

Reduce, Reuse, Recycle

Begin by reading the book *Just a Dream* by Chris Van Allsburg (Houghton Mifflin Co., 1990). Discuss the types of environmental damage found on each page of the dream sequence. Discuss how the boy does his part to help the environment.

Next, review the definitions of *recycling, reusing,* and *reducing.* Ask students to become aware every time they do something to help the environment. Provide an old shoe box (reuse) and have students decorate it with scraps of paper (reduce) from other projects. Tell them that every time they do something to help the environment, either at home or in school, they should write the actions on scrap pieces of paper and place them in the box. Post the headings" Reduce," "Reuse," and "Recycle" on a bulletin board. At the end of each week, read all entries and have students categorize them under the headings.

After working on this exercise for a few weeks, have each student write a journal entry about her experiences. Encourage her to write about the things that have changed in her daily routine in order to accomplish these tasks. Let students share their journal entries aloud.

Raising Awareness

Create a large display outside of the classroom where others can see your weekly efforts to help the environment. As a class, compose a letter to the school or local newspaper relating your activities about environmental awareness, and inviting visitors to see the display and interview students.

Record It

Purpose:

Young students should begin learning to write reports. Report writing is very different from the creative writing they are typically asked to do. This activity will help make report writing an enjoyable experience.

Reports Made Easy

Tailor this activity to a science unit. For example, if you are studying animals, have each student select one animal to study. Provide animal-related books and a list of Web sites. Immerse students in discussions about the animals, their features, environments, food sources, predators, and other interesting facts. Also, read a fictional animal story and discuss what makes it fiction. Then, share a report about an animal. Help them to see the differences and distinguish between the two types of writing.

Provide each student with a set of sentence starters below. Have students revisit the information they discovered about their animals and ask them to complete the sentence starters, draw pictures to go with some of the sentences, and use them to form the basis for the reports.

This report is about _____ .
Its size is _____ .
It looks _____ .
It has _____ .
It lives _____ .
It can move by _____ .
It likes to eat _____ .
Animals that attack it are _____ .
This animal is interesting because _____ .

Other Reports

Adapt the sentence starters to report writing in other subject areas. For example, focus on social studies by providing a different set of sequenced sentence starters about famous explorers. After practicing report writing over a period of time, students may only need key words rather than sentence starters.

What's the Problem?

Purpose:

Use students' curiosity about the world around them to inspire good science writing and problem solving.

Activity

Inquiring Minds Want to Hypothesize

Think about and share questions that could be tested scientifically, such as why one sock seems to disappear in the laundry, why sugar gets lumpy when left out, etc. Let each student write a list of questions. Collect the lists, then help each student choose an appropriate question to use for an experiment. (Materials should be easy to find, the test should be simple, etc.)

Let each student brainstorm ways he might answer his question. Have him write a few sentences about what he thinks the answer is and how he might test it. If students are ready, introduce the word *hypothesis*. Next, have each student write steps for an experiment he would like to perform to test his hypothesis. For example, if a student hypothesizes that socks get separated when laundry is sorted before it's washed, he could take a sock inventory for several loads of laundry before and after it is put into a washing machine, and before and after it is put into a dryer, to see when socks get separated. If a student hypothesizes that sugar gets lumpy when exposed to air, he could leave some out and put some into an air-tight container and compare them over a period of time.

Finally, allow students to use their science textbooks to learn how to properly set up and document experiments. Let students conduct their experiments for homework. When the experiments are complete, collect the data. Evaluate how closely students followed written procedures and how detailed their notes are, not whether their hypotheses are correct.

Extension

Parallel Experiments

Choose a few experiments with easy instructions and inexpensive materials to share with the class. Provide materials and copies of the students' procedures, without the hypotheses, for each pair of students. Have each pair write a new hypothesis and perform the experiment. (You may want to stagger them over several days.) Let students write their own experiment notes and document whether their results matched their hypotheses.

Capital Capitols

Purpose:

Students continually omit capital letters in their writing, and when you bring it to their attention they often say, "Oops," and forget the next time. To make connections between their writing and their knowledge of which words to capitalize more concrete, students should "spend time with capitals." Use your social studies curriculum to make the activity meaningful.

Book of Capitals

Devote a day, or even a week, to creating a capital letter booklet using proper nouns from your social studies reading. Let students staple lined pages together and write a letter of the alphabet on each page. Tell students to keep track of the capitalized words they come across in their social studies reading each day by writing them on corresponding letter pages in the booklets. For example, if students are learning about their home state or province or other states and provinces, capitols and other historic locations and people can be listed. At the end of each day or week, have students write summaries or stories of what they have learned using some or all of the words on their lists.

Capital "Venn-tures"

Post a large Venn diagram-type chart with three circles, one on the top and two on the bottom, arranged so that they overlap in the center. Label the circles "People," "Places," and "Things." As students find words that need to be capitalized, have them fill in the chart appropriately. Add examples of words that might fit in more than one category, such as Washington, which can be both a person and a place.

Capital King

At the end of each day, have students count up the number of capitalized words they found. Crown the student with the most words the "Capital King or Queen" of the day.

A Star Is Born

Social Studies

Purpose:

The following activity is great to complete at the beginning of the school year because it allows students to get to know each other. It's also a good review for writing essays.

Walk of Fame

Provide a large star pattern (about 18" or 46 cm across) for each student to trace onto heavy paper and cut out. Next, have each student write a "celebrity stat sheet" about herself, including details such as her full name, birthday, age, likes, dislikes, talents, and other personal information that would help others get to know her. Students should write paragraphs rather than make lists.

When the stars and stat sheets are finished, announce to the class that they will have a celebrity award ceremony and they will each get a star on your classroom walk of fame. Create a microphone from a cardboard tube and pass it to a student. Ask that student to be a "reporter." Give him a stat sheet. Have the writer of that stat sheet stand next to the "reporter" as he reads the autobiography and asks questions about it. As he does this, help the "star" sign her name on the bottom of the star, then use washable paint to make right and left handprints on the star above her signature. When students are finished, applaud and let the "reporter" choose the next "reporter," then have him become the next "star." When the stars are dry, laminate them and attach them to the floor or bulletin board, or attach to students' desks along with their stat sheets and leave them posted for an open house night.

Lives of the Famous

Have students use the Internet to research actual people whose names are on the real Walk of Fame. Let each student choose a favorite performer and submit it to you for approval. (Make sure all choices are appropriate.) Have students prepare stat sheets on their celebrities, including when the stars were designated, what accomplishments their celebrities have achieved, and other interesting biographical information. Let students present the reports to the class.

Dress-Up for Big Kids

Purpose:

Narrative writing is not always easy for students. Some students can write chapters, while others write only a few words. Keep students focused on writing with curriculum-related story prompts.

Activity

Theme-Day Themes

Plan a theme day related to current social studies curriculum and tell students that they will get to dress up and spend a day in character. Brainstorm ideas for the theme. For example, if students are studying their home state or province, let them brainstorm people and things that are important in that area. If students are studying a period in history, have them research people and things from that period.

Next, have each student choose a person or object and decide how to dress to represent what he chose. Costumes can be simple or elaborate. (Inanimate objects like the cotton gin or airplane can be interesting costumes!) Ask, "What would this person wear and why? What costume elements are necessary for others to know who or what you are?" Choose the date students will participate in theme day and help students with any costume concerns. You may wish to provide art supplies for students to work on their costumes in class, or assign them for homework and send notes to families.

On theme day, have students wear the costumes. Have students jot down ideas for stories their objects or characters might tell, then write stories about themselves as the characters. Have students share their stories aloud while wearing their costumes. To make theme day more interesting, before students reveal their identities, encourage them to guess others' characters or objects from the information in the stories.

Extensions

More Theme-Day Fun

Have students work in groups to write plays involving their characters or objects. How would they interact? How did they come to be together? Allow students to act out their plays.

Still More Theme-Day Fun

Have a backward day. Let students dress backward, run the class schedule backward, line up in reverse alphabetical order, and write backward stories.

Tried and True Traditions

Social Studies

Purpose:

Use literature and writing to help students understand each other better and learn different cultural traditions of their classmates.

My Family Does Things This Way

Begin this activity by reading the book *Chicken Sunday* by Patricia Polacco (PaperStar, 1998). Discuss the tradition of Pysanky eggs with students and research the art. (Intricately crafted Pysanky, or Easter, eggs are a Ukrainian tradition. The Ukraine in Eastern Europe is the second largest country after Russia.) Talk about traditions in your own family that you may do every year on a certain day. Encourage students to think about things they do with their families on special days or holidays.

For homework, have students discuss the traditions and their origins with their families. Why do they do them? What do they mean? Tell them that it is fine to call grandparents, other relatives, or friends (all with adult permission), or do research to get this information. Ask students to take notes.

Next, have students create posters of the traditions their families observe each year. Let students divide their posters into sections according to how many different traditions they observe. In each section, have a student state a tradition, draw a picture of himself or his family participating in it, or draw any symbols that represent that tradition and write one or two sentences stating why he does this and what it means. Allow students to share posters with the class and display for other classes to see.

Tradition Day

Have each student choose one tradition he can share with the class, such as a favorite holiday food, music, custom, etc. Be sure to get parents' permission and information about food allergies and religious or other food preferences before completing this activity. With parents' help, engage the class in these traditions. Encourage students to share any items or crafts that they use to observe the chosen tradition. Have each classmate write a thank-you note to the student telling what she liked about the shared tradition and why.

In Their Words

Social Studies

Purpose:

Students in this age group pay more and more attention to what people say in the world around them. Combine writing with history as they examine famous quotations.

My Favorite Quotations

Provide age-appropriate books or Web sites of famous quotations. Begin by talking about some of your favorite quotations. Tell each student to spend some time looking at Web sites or reading books and to choose three quotes that he finds interesting. For each quote, have him note the author of the quote and the source. (This is a good time to introduce citing sources.) As each student finds three quotes, have him take home the quotes he has copied and share them with family and friends. Then, he should choose one quote that makes a statement that he strongly believes in. It can be serious or funny, profound or lighthearted. After he chooses his quote, have him write it at the top of a sheet of paper and write one or two paragraphs below the quotation stating why he chose it and why he thinks it is important enough to remember. Instruct each student to sign his name at the bottom of his paper.

When students complete the activity, continue it in one of two ways. Collect the papers and cut off the top portions where the quotes are written. Mix up the quotes, number them, and post them on one side of a bulletin board. Label the paragraphs with letters (a, b, c, etc.) and post them on the other side. Let students read the quotes and descriptions and match them. Or, read each quote aloud and let students guess which classmate chose that quote. When someone guesses correctly, let the student who chose the quote read his paragraphs to the class, then select the next quote to be read aloud.

The Things We Say

Many teachers have collections of funny and interesting things their students have said through the years. Keep a quote wall in the classroom. Tape a sheet of bulletin board paper to a wall. As students say memorable things throughout the year, ask them to write these things like graffiti on the paper and sign their names. Before school ends for the summer, read the quotes from the quote wall to look back on the year.

Bio Picks

Social Studies

Purpose:

Teach students how to write biographies. Make it fun by letting students play a detective game at the end of the project.

Famous for What?

Begin by discussing what makes people famous. Talk about categories of famous people related to what students are studying, such as explorers, monarchs, presidents, inventors, painters, scientists, musicians, actors, poets, Nobel-prize winners, authors, etc. Ask each student to write down the names of two or three famous people and submit them you for approval. Eliminate choices until each student has one person to research and no celebrities are used twice. Next, let students research their people and write reports that will be presented to the class. Distribute the Bio Picks outline reproducible (page 49) for students to use.

When students have finished writing their reports, explain that each student must create a "jacket of clues" about his person for homework. Give each student a paper grocery bag. Each student should cut out arm and neck holes, and cut the front of the bag to make a jacket. On the inside flaps, have students write clues from their reports about the famous people they researched. Then, provide art supplies for each student to decorate the jacket to "suit" his famous person. For example, he could create a lab coat for a doctor or scientist, a robe for a king or queen, a uniform jacket for a general, etc.

Finally, designate a famous-people day. Display the jackets around the room. Let each student read his report aloud. Then, allow students to examine the jackets, read the clues inside them, and write down guesses to match them to the reports. (The time necessary to complete this activity will vary depending on students' ages and levels.)

Personality Parade

After students have finished guessing and the answers have been revealed, let students wear their jackets and read their reports to another class in their grade. Let the other class have a chance to guess what person each jacket represents.

Name_____ Date_____

Bio Picks Outline

Below is a list of questions you may want to research about your famous person. Write the answers on a separate piece of paper. Each question does not have to be answered. Because this is just a guide, your report should not answer these questions only. There will probably be other information you want to include in your report. Also, remember to write in paragraphs and to make your report as interesting as possible.

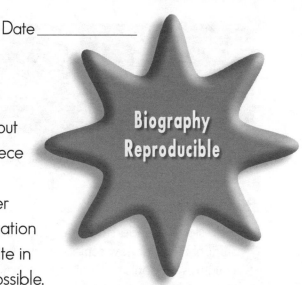

Biography Reproducible

Famous Person's Name: _____

Early Childhood

1. Where was the person born?
2. Where and by whom was this person raised?
3. What kind of life did this person have?

Education

1. Where did this person go to school?
2. What level of education did this person complete?
3. Who influenced this person as he or she was growing up?
4. Did school help this person achieve goals?

Accomplishments

1. Why is this person famous?
2. Have this person's accomplishments affected the world in any way?
3. Have this person's accomplishments affected your life directly?
4. How would the world be different if this person had never lived?

This Person's Life Today

1. Is this person alive today? If not, when did this person die?
2. How was this person's life changed by his or her accomplishments?
3. In your opinion, should this person be more or less famous than he or she is for these accomplishments? Why do you think so?

How Different Is It?

Purpose:

Help students understand the great sacrifice many people made to start new lives in a new world. Each student will interview someone who has lived in two different countries, then compare and contrast the countries. Students will write final essays and dedicate them to the people they interviewed.

There's No Place Like Home

Read the book *Grandfather's Journey* by Allen Say (Walter Lorraine Books, 1993). Explain that the man in the story left home to "see the world" but finally settled in California. Throughout the story he longs for the homeland he left behind. Have students compare and contrast California with Japan. Write responses on the board. Discuss how many people move to other countries for many reasons, and many of them come to North America. Just like the grandfather in the story, they sometimes miss their homelands, too.

Have each student find a relative, neighbor, or friend who has left his homeland to move to a new country. Tell students that they must have their families' permission before asking people to participate. Ask for volunteers to be interviewed by students who don't know anyone from another country. Have students work in groups to create interview questions. Remind them to include questions about things that are the same and different in the countries. Give students time to conduct their interviews.

When all students have found people to interview and have completed the assignment, ask each student to use her interview questions to write an essay about the person she interviewed. Ask her to include a dedication page to the person she interviewed. Have students read their stories to their classmates, then write thank-you notes to the people they interviewed. Have students mail their thank-you notes with the essays and dedications enclosed.

Where Would You Go?

Post a world map. As students read their essays aloud, indicate the different places they read about by placing pushpins on the map. When all students have presented, have each student choose a place from one of the essays, research it, and write about what it would be like to relocate there.

Banana Split

Cross-Curricular

Purpose:

Sequencing is an important skill for students to learn, and it is frequently addressed on standardized tests. When students give directions, repeat the steps for solving problems, or retell events in stories, they must use sequencing. There are many ways to reinforce sequencing. Below are a few activities students might enjoy.

Step-by-Step Splits

Be sure to get parents' permission and information about food allergies and religious or other food preferences before completing this activity. First, provide recipes for students to read so that they become familiar with the format. Discuss how recipe writing is different from other kinds of writing. Provide ingredients and materials for banana splits: bananas, ice cream, whipped topping, flavored syrup, maraschino cherries, bowls, spoons, ice-cream scoops, etc. Have each student draw and color a picture of a banana split, including only toppings she likes. Then, have her write directions to assemble it. Her writing should match the picture exactly and should be in recipe or list format. To check her work, let her trade directions (not drawings) with a classmate who should then assemble the treat from the directions only. Instruct students to follow the directions literally. For example, the directions should tell students what utensil to use to scoop ice cream, they should instruct students to remove lids if necessary, etc. If the directions are not exact, students may end up with disappointing banana splits! If there are glitches, give students a chance to add to their directions, copying them over if necessary. Make sure each student's directions enable her to have a treat before the assignment is complete.

More Food Fun

For homework, have students use the same method to write recipes for favorite foods they can prepare themselves—as they are preparing them. Even students who write about simple things, such as eating oranges or heating pizza in the microwave, will be surprised at how many steps there are.

Listen to This!

Purpose:

Having students write and sing songs can be an effective teaching tool. Students will often easily recall song lyrics. Encourage them to write songs for different lessons in class, such as remembering math facts, the scientific process, or the order of story or historical events.

Sing and Learn

Show (or sing) the following example to students to the tune of "Jingle Bells."

Mammals are warm-blooded,
And they feed their young.
Most are covered in
Hair or fur.
They breathe air through their lungs.

During a curriculum unit, have students brainstorm in groups and write songs about the events or facts to be remembered. Give each group a different event. Instruct students to choose familiar tunes to put with their songs. As each group writes a song, keep track of the tunes used so that there will be no repeats. Let each group practice singing. Then, on test-review day, give each group a turn teaching a song to the class. Review on subsequent days using the songs.

Modern Music

If students use this activity again, let students write raps of the information and share their raps at a classroom poetry session.

The Learning Board

Purpose:

Too often students go home after school, and when asked, "What did you learn today?" they respond, "Nothing." This activity will help them realize that they learn something new just about every day. Use this activity throughout the school year to show students, families, administrators, and even yourself the enormous amount of teaching and learning accomplished daily.

Posting Knowledge

Begin by designating a bulletin board or an area of the room where "The Learning Board" can be set up year-round. Divide the board into subject areas depending on what you teach. Affix a subject area title at the top of each section. At the end of each day or week, have each student choose a colorful index card on which to write what she has learned, her name, and the date, and attach it under the appropriate heading.

At the end of the month, remove all learning cards and start again. Keep the cards for a huge review at the end of the year. Students will be quite impressed with all that they have learned, and you will be, too! As students look back through the cards, let each student choose one and write a paragraph about why it was an important thing to learn and how that knowledge has helped her.

Knowledge Party

Consider inviting families to a learning board party where students can showcase knowledge they gained throughout the year. Group cards by subject and post them around the room. If there is time to prepare, let students write learning-card questions for their parents. Quiz parents and let them try to find the posted answers.

Time-Capsule Writing

Purpose:

Let students use writing to reflect and keep records of important things that happen during the school year. They will see how much their lives have changed in a year's time, as well as how much better their writing has become.

Big Events

Provide a large box with a lid for students to cover with paper and decorate. Write "Time Capsule" on the lid. Secure the lid to the box with packing tape and cut a slit in the lid. Place the box near your desk. Next, with family permission, photograph each student participating in a school activity, such as working on a science experiment, participating in a school play, displaying an art project, or just working or eating lunch. Distribute the photographs and have each student write a few paragraphs explaining what she is doing in the photograph and how it related to what was happening in her life at the time. Have her sign and date the back of the photograph and the writing. Attach the photograph to the writing and place it in the box. Make sure you contribute photos of your own, and consider allowing students to take them!

Near the end of the school year, open the time capsule and return the photographs and writing to students. Have each student read her paragraphs, look at the pictures, and write an essay about how looking back in time makes her feel. If possible, take another photograph of each student so that she can compare how different she looks. Let volunteers share their writing with the class.

Taking Inventory

Periodically have students write "life inventory" paragraphs about who their friends are, which school subjects are their most and least favorites, their addresses, what they have learned recently, etc. Each time a student writes a "capsule entry," have him sign and date it, place it in an envelope, write his name and the date on the envelope, and seal it. Collect envelopes and store them in the time capsule. Have students write their last entries at least one month before the end of the school year.

If I Could Talk . . .

Purpose:

This lesson can be adapted to most curriculum areas. It is an effective assessment tool, a good content review, and best of all, students will have fun completing it.

Story of an Object

With personification, a student can take whatever she is studying, bring it to life, and tell its story. For example, if students are studying the planets, have each student choose one planet and personify it by writing a paragraph in first person to tell what she knows about her planet. For this assignment, a student might write, " Hi! My name is Mercury. I am the closest planet to the sun. I am less than half the size of Earth. I have craters just like Earth's moon. If you lived on me, you would get to have a birthday every 88 Earth days. That's how long it takes me to orbit around the sun. Unfortunately, each day for me is equal to 59 days on Earth. That's a long day! Because I have little atmosphere to block out the sun's heat, sometimes my temperature reaches over 800° F (427° C). That's pretty hot. But, I love being the first planet in a long line of great planets. My closest neighbor is Venus."

Possible math topics could be operation signs, prime numbers, measurement, and geometric shapes. Possible science topics could be plants, animals, atoms, electricity, thermometers, simple machines, engines, water, tides, rocks, pollution, celestial bodies, parts of the body, bodies of water, geographical places (such as rain forests, mountains, the poles, etc.). Possible social studies topics could be capitol buildings, historical documents, courtrooms, battlefields, historical landmarks, countries' flags, states or provinces, bills or laws, or local landmarks.

Act It Out

If you have students choose their topics around a unit of study, form groups of students with closely related topics to write and perform skits. For example, if students are studying astronomy, form four groups: planets, stars and constellations, Earth and moon, and comets and meteorites.

Your Wish Is Granted

Purpose:

Students are often asked what they would wish for if given three wishes, and usually they wish for money, games, candy, etc. This activity is more focused and will provide students with the opportunity to think about wishes that will affect their community, state or province, and country.

My Wish Is . . .

Tell each student to imagine that she is walking along the beach when she notices something shiny hidden in the sand. When she picks it up, she finds that it is a glass bottle covered in maps. She rubs it to clean it off, when out pops Nate, the Genie of Nations. He tells her that she has three very specific wishes: one for her town, one for her state or province, and one for her country. What will each student wish for?

Have each student brainstorm a list of things that would make her town, state or province, and country better places to live. From that list, have her select those that she thinks would benefit the most people and write about them. For each, she should include her wish, why she chose it, and how and who it will affect. Students should share their wishes with classmates. Consider sending their wishes in the form of friendly letters to a relevant political leader or local newspaper editorial page.

More Wishes

This idea can be used across all curriculum areas. Create your own or consider the following "genies" for various subjects.

Caesar, the Genie of History: Select three wishes that would change three events in history.

Einstein, the Genie of Science: Select three wishes that would change things in science or medicine.

Stork, the Genie of Children: Select three wishes that would affect children only.

Leo, the Genie of Animals: Select three wishes that would affect only animals.

Did You Know?

Purpose:

In upper-elementary grades, students are often asked to write expository paragraphs that give information about topics. Just like in story writing, students need to organize their thoughts, order their sentences, and use words like *first, second, third,* and *finally.* This activity will take students through the steps necessary to write clear, organized, expository paragraphs.

Step by Step

Give students a list of curriculum-related topics for their paragraphs. For example, if they are studying Native North Americans, have students write about the steps involved in building a particular traditional, tribal home. If they are studying electricity, ask students to write the steps necessary to build a complete circuit. In math, you might ask students to give directions to complete a long-division problem. If you prefer more general topics, consider topics like following school-bus procedures, writing notes to a substitute teacher to explain the daily routine, training a puppy, following rules for Internet safety, etc.

When students have chosen their topics, begin by having them write topic sentences. Next, have them list steps or important events they want to include in their paragraphs. Then, have students order their steps using transition words (*first, second, then,* etc.). Finally, have students write first drafts of their paragraphs, and follow the Writing Process Checklist (page 61) to complete this activity.

Transitioning to Good Writing

During the course of this activity, have students brainstorm transition and relational words. Put students into groups and assign topics for their transition words, such as words that show order or time, words that show place or location, words that compare and contrast things, or words to begin a concluding paragraph or sentence. Have each group create a chart to display in the classroom for future reference.

Guest Speaker

Cross-Curricular

Purpose:

Public speaking is an important skill. Students must continually practice in order to feel comfortable. Writing good speeches can help students feel more confident when it is their turn to speak in front of the class.

It's My Turn to Talk

Provide famous speeches for students to read, or have them research speeches on the Internet, such as excerpts from Martin Luther King, Jr.'s "I Have a Dream" speech or Lou Gehrig's "Farewell to Baseball" speech. Write the list on the board and let students share parts of the speeches. Ask students what made these speeches so memorable. Discuss the content and the delivery of each speech. Explain that most speeches teach, inform, or persuade.

Inform each student that he will be writing and delivering one of each of these three types of speeches. Set time limits for each speech, possibly one to two minutes for the first speech and three to five minutes for the second and third speeches. Begin with a demonstration (teaching) speech so that students have opportunities to write about things that are familiar to them. Encourage them to bring in props for their demonstration speeches.

Have each student use the Guest Speaker Outline reproducible (page 59) to organize his speech. Next, he should write out his speech, then revise and edit it until it is within the time frame provided. Finally, each student should write the key points of his speech on index cards to use while he is presenting. When students have given their first speeches, provide feedback and start the process again for the second and third types of speeches. Help students think of speech topics that are relevant to them.

Feedback Forum

Teach students to write responses to each other's speeches. Discuss criteria for evaluating speeches, such as making eye contact, speaking clearly, etc. Give each student a stack of index cards. As a student begins her speech, have each classmate write her name at the top of one index card. After she gives the speech, have each classmate write two positive things on the card and one area for improvement.

Name_____ Date_____

Guest Speaker Outline

Below is a list of tasks you need to complete in order to write your speech. Use this sheet to remember the steps.

1. Choose a specific topic that interests you. Your speech will be better if you feel strongly about your topic.
    My topic is _____ .

2. Gather information from books, magazines, encyclopedias, the Internet, personal experience, or interviews with experts. Use at least two references.
    My references are _____
    _____
    _____ .

    From your research, choose important information you want to include in your speech and cross out information that you think should not be in your speech.

3. Order the information so that your speech has a beginning, middle, and end, and you have included everything you wanted to say.
    A. _____
    B. _____
    C. _____
    D. _____
    E. _____
    F. _____

4. Choose an attention-getting topic sentence so that the audience listens to what you say.
    My topic sentence is _____
    _____ .

5. Write your speech on a separate sheet of paper. Use the Writing Process Checklist (page 61) to revise and edit your writing until it is interesting and easy to understand. Practice reading your speech until you have memorized it. Then, practice speaking clearly and with expression. Finally, practice your speech with your family or a friend. Remember to make eye contact.

6. Jot down the key points of your speech on an index card so that you can glance at it to help you smoothly deliver your speech.

Worth a Thousand Words

Purpose:

Keep students interested in writing by varying the lengths of assignments. For example, demonstrate that a simple poster, using just a few words and pictures, can send a strong message.

 ctivity

Posters with the Most

Prior to this activity, collect various posters that send strong messages. Borrow posters from other teachers or gather several poster catalogs for students to browse. Display the posters you have collected. Discuss the important elements in each poster, such as pictures, sayings, colors, layout, etc., as well as the meaning of each poster. Ask if students think the poster is effective. Why or why not?

Next, ask students to brainstorm well-known slogans and jingles, including some they see on the posters. Examples might be campaigns about recycling, preventing forest fires, favorite foods and beverages, etc. Discuss the meaning of each slogan found on the posters. Then, challenge students to create slogans of their own. If you want students to keep their ideas less commercial, have them think in categories such as prejudice, education, health, animal rights, environmentalism, sportsmanship, anticrime, antidrug, etc. Finally, have students create posters with their own sayings. Talk with each student about artwork and space planning to make sure the message is clear, and allow him to make a first draft of his work. Provide poster board and art supplies for students to create their posters. Display the posters around the room and have a gallery day for students to walk around the classroom and look at the posters. Next to each poster, attach a half sheet of paper on which students may write positive comments. Consider displaying posters in a hallway or library.

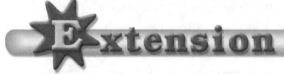 xtension

Jingle Writing

Let students write jingles to familiar tunes that tie in with the posters they have drawn. Give examples of familiar jingles for popular products. Students will recognize ads for child-friendly foods and toys. Let each student present her poster and jingle to the class, then lead the class in singing the jingle.

Writing Process Checklist

Follow these steps to produce better writing. This process
works with almost any assignment.

Prewriting: This is the first step in writing essays, paragraphs, stories
speeches, poetry, and reports.

_____ I have brainstormed my entire piece of writing, including a plot,
setting, characters, organization, and conclusion. (Use only those that
are appropriate.)

_____ I have completed the research I needed.

_____ I have a beginning, middle, and end.

First Draft: This is the part of the writing process where you write without worrying about grammar
and spelling. Use any words you want to use.

_____ I have used my prewriting ideas to write.

_____ I have included details to make my writing interesting.

Revising: This important step in the writing process helps you think about your writing again. Does it
do what you want it to do?

_____ I have a good topic sentence for each paragraph.

_____ I have put my writing in an effective sequence.

_____ I have used enough details.

_____ I have used a dictionary or thesaurus to find more interesting words.

_____ I have added words and sentences where they are needed.

_____ I have deleted words and sentences where they are not needed.

Editing: This is the part of the writing process where you must carefully read your story several times
and look for mistakes.

_____ I have used the Editing Checklist to check for errors in sentence structure, capitalization,
punctuation, and spelling.

_____ At least two friends or family members have proofread my story.

Final Draft: This is the last part of the writing process. Use your best handwriting or type your writing
on a computer.

_____ I have used my best handwriting.

_____ I have run spell check on my typed paper.

_____ My story is neat and easy to read.

Writing
Process
Reproducible

Editing Checklist

Use the following checklist when editing a piece of writing.

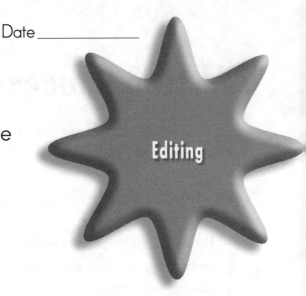

Editing

Did I use correct sentence structure?

____ I used complete sentences.

____ I have no sentence fragments.

____ I made my sentences interesting.

____ I combined short, choppy sentences.

Did I use transitional words to show the order of my writing?

____ I used words like *first, next, then, later, finally,* etc., where needed.

____ I helped my readers understand the order of events in my story.

Did I use the best language to get my point across?

____ I used descriptive adjectives and adverbs.

____ I used the correct nouns and verbs. They agree in number.

Did I use capital letters correctly?

____ I started each sentence with a capital letter.

____ I used capital letters to start proper nouns and titles.

Did I use correct punctuation?

____ I ended each sentence with the correct punctuation mark.

____ I used commas correctly.

____ I used quotation marks to show characters speaking.

____ I used apostrophes in contractions.

Did I spell my words correctly?

____ I checked to make sure all words were spelled correctly.

____ I checked to make sure I used the correct words.

Journal Writing

Purpose:

Cross-curricular journal writing is a good way for students to receive extra writing practice. Below are a few ideas that will make journal writing more meaningful to students.

Center Idea

Encourage Creativity

Have students create journals. In a center, store craft materials for students to use to make journals, such as markers, paints, tagboard for covers, different types of paper, etc. Allow them to choose the shapes, sizes, and designs. Encourage them to think of creative yet effective ways to bind the journals.

Activities

Perfect Predictions

At the beginning of the year, have students write lists of predictions. Possible predictions could be who will win a national or local election, who will win a sports championship, whether the groundhog will see his shadow, how many snow or bad weather days there will be this year, etc. At the end of the year, revisit the predictions. Give a prize to the student with the most correct predictions.

Learning Log

Let students use their journals to reflect on what they have learned and what they still need to learn. Students can write chapter summaries, pre-reading questions, open-ended questions about lessons, and even suggestions for you about what they would like to be taught again or differently. Collect the journals, respond to them, and use the feedback to inspire future lessons.

Go for the Goal

Use journal writing to have students look toward the future and set goals. For a beginning-of-the-year assignment, have each student write three personal goals and three school-related goals. For example, personal goals might be trying out for a team, keeping a clean room, staying physically active, etc. School-related goals could be learning long division, improving handwriting, learning to type, getting a good conduct grade, etc. Have students write their goals on the inside covers of their journals and check them off as they accomplish them.

Topical Solution

If some students feel that they are just "not good" in certain subject areas, raise confidence levels with journal activities. First, let each student write about why he doesn't feel confident in an area. Have him write a journal entry to you whenever he feels "lost." Reply to each student with encouragement and suggestions for improvement. Also, pair each student with a partner who excels in that area. Let the pair pass their journals back and forth, writing about different aspects of the subject area. Students will begin to gain confidence through repeated exposure to and conversation about their weak areas.

Journal Writing Mini-Unit

I Want to Know!

Ask each student to designate the last 10 pages in her journal to keep a record of this ongoing entry assignment. In this section, periodically have students write about the things they would like to learn in school but never do. Entries may be serious or funny. Check these entries occasionally and use them to plan special lessons.

Testing 1, 2, 3

Use journals to get test feelings out in the open. After a review for a test, ask students to write questions they think should be on the test. Or, have students write letters to you about how they would like to review for tests. Have students write about their feelings as soon as they finish their tests, then discuss their entries in the context of helping them do better the next time.

Conflict Resolution

Let students use journals to reflect on class situations. If a disagreement arises between several students, have students write about possible compromises or solutions to the dilemma. For example, if several students misbehave to the point of having silent lunch, let them write about how it made them feel and what they could do differently next time.

So Critical!

Explain the job of a critic by sharing film, music, book, game, and restaurant reviews. Have students pretend they are critics. Ask each student to critique one of the options mentioned above or a school assembly. Require that each thing being reviewed should be experienced within the week of the assignment. Let students read their critiques aloud.

Prompt Jar

Instead of struggling to write your own writing prompts, use students' creativity to do the job. After students have experience writing to prompts, give each student five index cards and tell him to write a prompt on each card. Collect the cards and discard any that are inappropriate. Fold each card several times and place it in a jar with a lid. Then, when it is time for students to write in their journals, let one student draw a prompt from the jar and read it aloud. Or, let each student draw a prompt, tape it to a journal page, and respond to it.

Dear Diary

Have each student pretend her journal is a diary. At the end of the day, have each student write a diary entry about her day in school.